PICTURES FROM THE ARCHIVES OF

Stockport
Express & Times

STOCKPORT
FLASHBACK

PICTURES FROM THE ARCHIVES OF
Stockport
Express & Times

STOCKPORT FLASHBACK

COMPILED BY CHRIS HILL

breedon **books**
PUBLISHING

First published in Great Britain in 2002 by
The Breedon Books Publishing Company Limited
Breedon House, 3 The Parker Centre,
Derby, DE21 4SZ.

ISBN 1 85983 338 1

Printed and bound by Butler & Tanner, Frome, Somerset, England.

Cover printing by Lawrence-Allen Colour Printers, Weston-super-
Mare, Somerset.

Contents

Introduction   7

Times Past   8

Hard News   75

Pictures Royal   93

Politicians in Focus   109

Famous Faces   118

Aviation in Stockport   133

Military Matters   147

Sporting Stockport   156

YOU in the picture   170

Introduction

THE idea to compile a contemporary pictorial history of Stockport was born from another venture to display images of our town and its people – a photographic exhibition in the town's principal art gallery. In fact, the underlying concept in both enterprises is an attempt to put something back into the communities our newspapers have served... an enjoyable means of saying thank you to our readership.

While much of the work in this book – and, indeed, the exhibition staged in September/October 2002 – is unashamedly nostalgic, it presents an evocation of the events and defining moments that have shaped this town's recent history and established its place in 21st-century Britain.

But this is not necessarily a history book, rather a compilation of images than can largely be enjoyed in themselves. The reader need not be from Stockport to appreciate these snapshots of the town.

Stockport Flashback is a heritage collection of photographs taken mostly by the very people who each week document our town's life – the photographers of the *Stockport Express and Stockport Times*. It is their industry, often under the pressure of meeting deadlines, that has produced the enduring work that features in *Stockport Flashback*. So while the archives have been plundered to produce this book, many of its pages feature images well within the memory of many younger Stopfordians. This is press photography first and foremost... the news in pictures from the last 50 or so years. We have pulled together prints of royal visits, changing landscape, people and places, events major and minor.

Our thanks must be expressed to the patient and co-operative staff of Stockport Heritage Library and of our own librarian Liz Pearce, who have helped enormously in the compilation of this work. But particular recognition must be given to the dedication and enthusiasm of Chris Hill, picture editor of the *Stockport Express and Stockport Times*, without whom this book would not have been so thorough, diverse and enjoyable.

Stewart Rigby,
Editor,
Stockport Express and Stockport Times

Times Past

Travis Brow pictured in 1874. George's Road is going off the picture to the right. Travis Brow is centre and Brinksway is the road going to the left. The photographer would have his back towards what was known as the Gardener's Arms Inn.

St Petersgate and High Street in the 1890s.

Wellington Bridge (right) on Wellington Road in the late 1880s or early 1890s. Right of the picture is where Merseyway precinct is now. This picture was originally printed from a glass plate that had broken diagonally. The photographer had tried to put the two pieces together, but had left the two halves out of line. With the help of modern computer manipulation we reconstructed the damage. The join can be seen slightly in the posters, but it is now back as the original photographer intended.

The first *Express* office, on the corner of Lord Street and Wellington Street in the 1890s. Notice the printers in their traditional aprons.

The opening of the Salvation Army citadel on Hillgate in 1895.

Nelstrops Flour Mill workers, Lancashire Hill, in 1895.

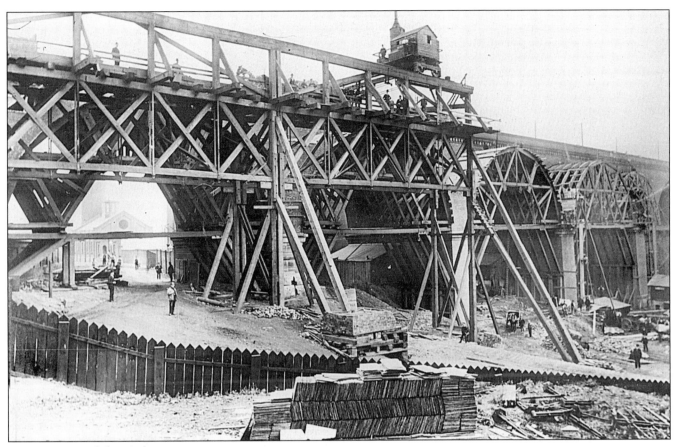

Construction of the viaduct.

Stockport's most famous landmark was treated to a facelift during the 1990s. Brickwork was cleaned and restored in what proved to be a mammoth task. The section that was added in the accompanying 1888 picture can be seen on the left.

These gentlemen are perhaps a little overdressed to attend a bonfire to celebrate the Diamond Jubilee of Queen Victoria in 1897, but without doubt they have made a splendid sartorial effort for the occasion! This original sepia print was found in our archives in a very faded (almost invisible) condition, and a little work with the computer has made it possible to see these proud toffs again.

Another group of superbly suited gentlemen outside what was known as the Hole in the Wall pub, Bridge Street Brow (leading to Stockport Market). We are uncertain of the date but the flags might indicate Queen Victoria's Silver Jubilee or the Coronation of George V in 1911.

Norbury Sunday School procession. Hazel Grove, 1906.

Front page of the *County Borough Express* in 1908. Note the advertisements for a rail excursion to Torquay – eight and half hours non-stop – and the Grand demonstration in aid of the Crimea and Indian Mutiny veterans. It cost the reader half of an old penny for this printed enlightenment. – no pictures though!

Plenty of stock in the windows of Bramhall Lane Post Office as these ladies (and dog) pose for a photograph.

Bradshaw's Boot Repairer's and Clogger's at 8 Gilmore Street, Shaw Heath, pictured in 1910.

Stockport Sunday School Walk, 1906.

Another scene of the 1906 Stockport Sunday School Walk of Witness. It must have been a nice day as the umbrellas seem to be used to protect the walkers from the sun. Or perhaps they were hedging their bets!

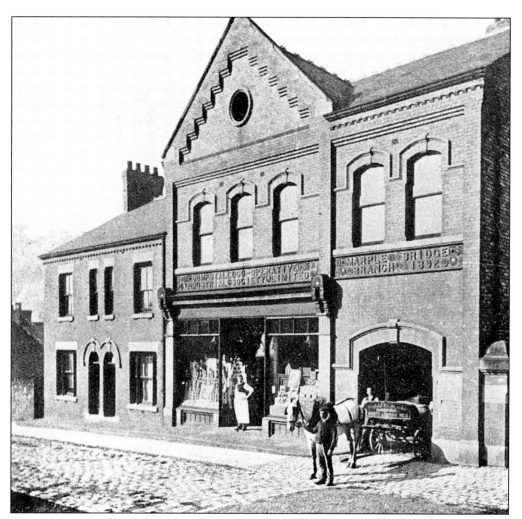

A horse-drawn delivery leaves the Marple Bridge branch of the Compstall Co-operative Industrial Society. This building still exists complete with the brick lettering over the shop. Unfortunately it is not stocked with fine cheeses and provisions served by a gentleman in a clean white apron!

When trains were on time – a steam train pulls into Davenport station in 1912. This picture was used by the *Stockport Advertiser* in 1964 for a nostalgia article, and suggested that the lady seated left was a Mrs Carlise of Buxton, who sold eggs in the Davenport area for many years.

Bygone times on Heaton Lane – now Princess Street.

This is an idyllic scene of Reddish Vale in 1915. Photograph was taken from the top of Reddish Vale Road near the entrance to Reddish Vale School.

Industrial smoke-stained frontage of Stockport Infirmary in the 1920s. Opened in 1834 it was closed in 1996 with the façade retained and cleaned to its original condition, with a totally new development at the rear.

Stockport Masonic Hall and Club, Greek Street. Stockport Photographic Society moved into these premises for a period, but apparently the installation of a darkroom led to a flood in the building!

An outing from Cale Green Reform Club. We wonder where they were going – Marple Roman Lakes perhaps? We are uncertain of the date.

A proud conductor stands to attention for the photographer, together with the first Stockport Corporation Tramways motor omnibus, 1919.

Horse-drawn tram from Stockport to Hazel Grove. Not the fastest mode of transport, but considering modern levels of traffic congestion on the A6, Dobbin and Daisy (names of the horses, not the men) would have got to Hazel Grove quicker than any current transport.

Stockport Corporation Tramways pose for a picture.

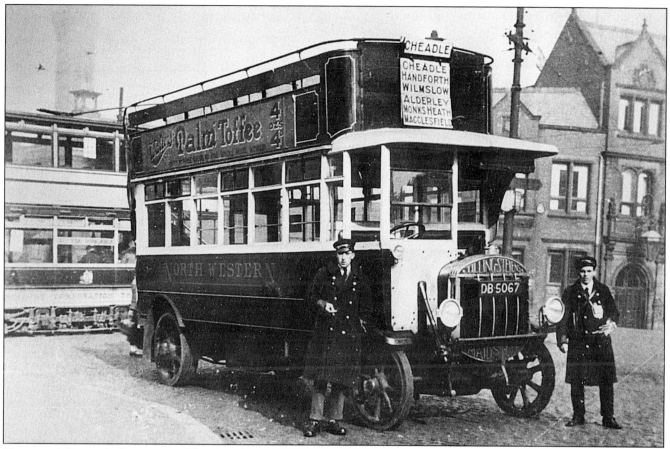

You certainly needed overcoats like this driver and conductor to ride on the open top deck of this North Western omnibus, pictured before departing for Cheadle from Mersey Square in the 1920s.

A Stockport Corporation tram outside the Blossoms Hotel. The destination board on the side of the tram is marked, Stockport-Dialstone Lane-Hazel Grove. In the future the introduction of Metro routes to Stockport will see this mode of transport come full circle.

This single-decker in the 1930s is heading for Parrs Wood, from Mersey Square. (When the driver arrives!)

Hazel Grove station was opened in June 1857. But the low platforms shown on the picture were a continual source of complaint. One critic, said that ladies had to be 'lifted down like a sack of potatoes'. The station was altered and extended in 1875 but the platforms were not raised until some time later.

A Stockport Corporation Tramways wagon, complete with driver in a magnificent uniform, outside the fire station in Mersey Square, *c*.1920s. It is possible that the man in the picture is actually a fireman.

Stockport Fire Station in 1910. The gleaming new *Mary Dalziel* fire engine, pictured on the right, was to replace the horse-drawn engines.

Those were the days – no traffic and you can park your horse and cart anywhere! Cheadle village, High Street.

Same scene of Cheadle High Street in modern times. There is also very little traffic on this picture. It must have been a Sunday!

Schools Hill junction of Wilmslow Road, Cheadle, a peaceful corner in days past to rest during a cycle ride. The gates on the left of the photograph were the entrance to the old Moseley Hall School which is long gone. But the gates still exist.

Local youth in Cheadle Village. The George and Dragon pub is pictured left.

The White Hart pub, High Street, Cheadle, decorated for the Coronation in 1911.

Pictured in 1977 – Abney Hall, Cheadle.

A tram trundles towards Stockport from Cheadle. This bridge is where a roundabout now takes you to the M60 slip-road.

Old Bell and Co's (the company taken over by Robinson's Brewery) Oddfellows pub, Heaton Lane.

An era when EVERBODY wore hats or caps. A football match crowd where Stockport's most famous product is in evidence without exception.

Almost a ready-made film set for the offices of Marley and Scrooge in *A Christmas Carol*. This building was on St Peter's Square, where Intoto Kitchens now have showrooms, opposite St Peter's Church. With apologies if the company depicted in the photograph still exists – I am sure you now allow your clerks more coal on the fire during the winter!

Crowther Street, off Hillgate, Stockport. A drawing by Lowry in 1930 called *Crowther's Buildings* (courtesy of Bonhams Auctioneers, London).

The same scene that inspired Lowry's 1930 drawing, *Crowther's Buildings*. We guess the drawing and photograph were done at about the same period.

Lowry drawing, *Stockport Viaduct*, dated 1943.
(courtesy of Bonhams Auctioneers, London).

A Lowryesque picture – Lowry actually did a pencil
drawing of this scene in 1943 looking towards the
viaduct, complete with a steam train (see above).

Pear Mill Ladies swimming team, 1933.

Stockport Premier juvenile morris dancers, 1924.

We are uncertain of the date of this picture found in our files. In the foreground are some allotments, which must be in the vicinity of what is now the area near B&Q and Decathlon stores.

Street party in Somers Road, Reddish, for the 1937 Coronation of King George VI. Our file picture gave credit to 'Mr E. Crapper the well-known local photographer'.

'Something I said?' A lone figure poses for the camera in the labyrinth of World War Two air-raid shelters cut from the sandstone into the side of Chestergate. They are now open as a tourist attraction for visitors.

This picture inside the Chestergate air-raid shelter looks authentic 1942. It was actually taken during 1992 as a mock-up. Pictured are Jo Hague, and Vic Barry with their WRVS tea stall.

Vandalism in 1944 was usually only the work of the Luftwaffe. This staff picture was passed for publication by the Press and Censorship Bureau, and blandly captioned: 'A solitary bomb robbed the green of its orderliness'. We are uncertain where this bowling green is actually situated.

Nield and Hardy, Great Underbank, in the 1950s. This demolished building was next to the existing timbered National Westminster Bank, selling state-of-the-art televisions of the period.

Hanover Chapel (now demolished), Tiviot Dale, in the 1950s.

A Stockport industrial scene taken during the 1950s which has vanished almost completely. Faulder's Mill can be seen (centre) together with the power station (right) and the cooling tower dominating the whole town. Photograph was taken from Tiviot Dale station which, like the skyline, has long since gone.

A cobbled Mersey Square in the early 1950s.

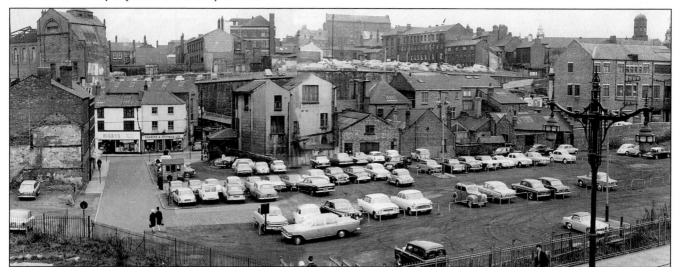

This early 1960s photograph, taken before the construction of Merseyway Precinct, was filed in our archives as two separate prints. They have been now digitally joined. Note the cars... all now a collector's dream.

Suburban chimneys with tell-tale signs of roaring coal fires were a common sight, as can be seen from this picture, looking over house backs towards the power station in the 1950s.

Junction of Princes Street and Mersey Square, late 1950s. Just park and shop!

Little Mill Inn, Rowarth, in the 1950s. Essentially this scene has changed little and Rowarth is still a pleasant venue for a summer's evening pint (or two).

Winter's Jewellers, Great Underbank, early 1950s.

Underbank some 15 years later from the opposite direction. This is now a pedestrian area closed to traffic. Most of the business signs have now changed, and Winter's is now a bar.

Mersey Square in the early 1950s. The Plaza cinema is showing *The Solid Gold Cadillac* – not many of those on Stockport's streets in those austere times!

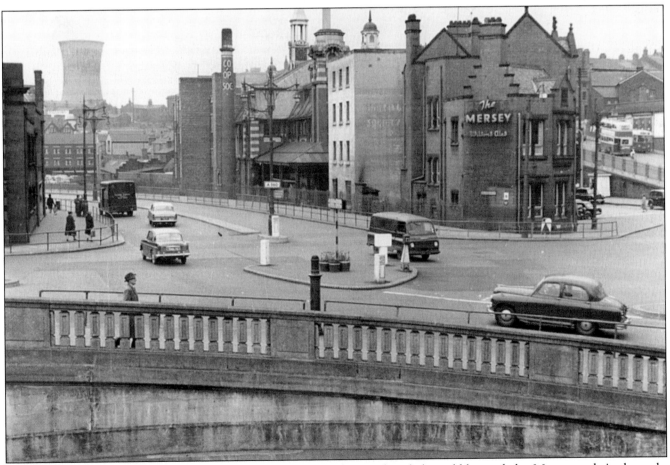

A later picture of Mersey Square possibly *c.*1960 Tarmac has replaced the cobbles and the Mersey pub is the only building to survive into the 21st century.

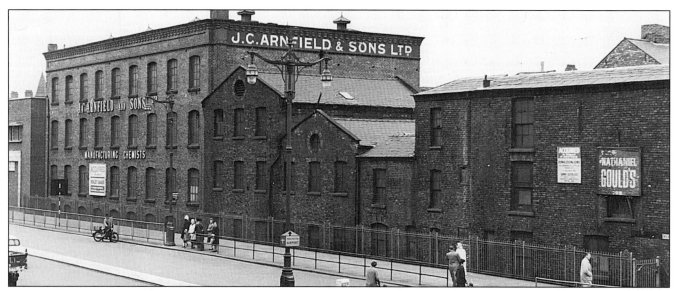

Another view of Merseyway in the late 1950s or early 1960s.

The power station cooling tower and mill chimneys dominate this stark, unforgiving industrial panorama of Stockport during the 1960s. Most of these features are now long gone – undoubtedly for the better.

Andrew Square demolition, looking towards the Parish Church in the 1960s. We wonder how many *Stockport Express* editions were sold from the hut in the foreground. It was there for many years.

Stockport Corporation Transport Social Club, pictured on the right of this viaduct scene from the mid-1960s. This club moved to what is now the Masters snooker centre on Wood Street, Hollywood. Note from the advertisement on the side of the nearest bus that Nelson tipped cigarettes were 3s 6d (17½p) for a pack of 20!

Cheadle Station closed in 1964 and became a pub.

Viaduct in the late 1960s-early '70s. Mill chimneys were fast disappearing from the skyline, but these giants of the industrial revolution were all to fall at the hands of the demolition experts.

Junction of Princes Street and Wellington Road North, 1964. Debenhams is now bottom right where the Touchstone pub is pictured with the white chimneys. The bus depot (top right) was demolished and is now a car park, but you can still buy a pint in the George pub (centre left).

This photograph taken from the old Fire Station tower (where the front of Merseyway precinct now stands), illustrates what a Dickensian industrial wasteland the heart of our town was at this period (1950s-60s). On the left is Wellington Road North (A6) and Debenhams now stands in the foreground.

Junction of Lancashire Hill, Sandy Lane, Manchester Road and Belmont Way in the early 1970s. On the right of the photograph is where the roundabout and Wickes store is now. The chimney pictured was eventually demolished by Fred Dibnah.

Work starting on the roundabout on the Lancashire Hill, Sandy Lane and Manchester Road junction in the early 1970s.

A panda police car patrols Castle Street, Edgeley, in the early 1960s.

King Street West, early 1960s.

Another view of Daw Bank looking towards the viaduct in the late 1960s. This open-air museum for scrap 1950s Ford motor cars is now the home of Stockport's bus station.

Dumped scrap cars were a real problem in the late 1960s. Daw Bank (where the bus station is now) became the end of the road for this 1950s Ford Pop and its companions. Houses ready for demolition in the background are on Chestergate with the viaduct to the left, just off the picture.

Dangerous adventure playground for these two children, but no doubt they spent many happy hours pretending they were driving a shiny new limo to the seaside. Picture used during 1967 to illustrate the problems of dumped cars.

A magnet for young children – this scrap Standard Van was dumped on Blackberry Lane, Brinnington, in 1967. These children will be over 40 years old now!

Stockport Advertiser building in the 1960s. Established in 1822 it was the main competitor to the *Stockport Express* until the advent of free-sheets and the need for large scale investment forced it into *Manchester Evening News* ownership. The *Advertiser* title was eventually incorporated into our company as the *Express Advertiser,* but the name is now defunct.

Below: Daw Bank car and bus park in 1978, the site of the present bus station. Do you wish we had the same town centre parking facility now?

Last gas lamp in Stockport being removed. Manvers Street (off Sandy Lane), Reddish, in the 1960s. Note the small dog mourning the demise of its favourite 'relieving post'.

A high level picture of Stockport town centre, taken late 1970s early '80s. Obviously a clear day as the hills towards Marple can be seen.

Gone, but not forgotten – the Essoldo and Super cinemas in the early 1950s.

A later photograph of the Essoldo taken in the 1960s – not a Japanese car in sight!

Popular as ever – a busy Stockport market in the early 1960s.

Those were the days – very little traffic and you could park your car anywhere. Merseyway early 1960s.

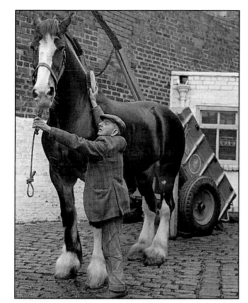

Duke, one of Robinson's Brewery's dray horses, on the verge of his retirement in January 1976. Dray horses are still used for promotional and light work with the brewery.

Merseyway in the early 1970s. Note the looming presence of the power station cooling tower. Buildings on the left of the photograph have all been demolished to extend the shopping precinct.

A view seldom seen – concrete arches that support the precinct over the River Mersey in 1980.

Old Stockport – a stark picture of the Huntsman's Brow area, Heaton Norris, prior to demolition. Deserted cobbles that will evoke memories of countless families who lived their lives here in 1973.

Demolition of Huntsman's Brow, Stockport, in 1973.

A cobbled Wood Street. Now home for the *Stockport Express and Times* it is one of the main routes from the town centre to the M60, complete with regular police speed checks, using the latest hi-tech equipment. Such checks would be pointless in this sleepy scene from the 1960s.

Wood Street in present times. Traffic rushes in a constant stream towards the Pyramid roundabout and M60 junction.

The Brinksway Pictorium, pictured in the 1980s.

These house were off New Zealand Road and were demolished in 1972. The picture will bring back many memories for people who spent their lives there.

Washing day on Gorsey Bank Estate. Obviously one of those sunny days when every housewife sets to work before the weather turns nasty. Old pram wheels in the foreground are a little boy's dream for constructing a go-kart or bogey – difficult to find now.

Meal House Brow (between Great Underbank and the Market) in the 1960s. In the 1970s the café became a greengrocer's for a short while. This building used to be Stockport's first police station.

Construction of the multi-storey car park, Heaton Lane.

Laying the ground for the construction of the multi-storey car park, Heaton Lane.

'Welcome to the Bronx' – urban decay in Adswood in the early 1980s.

Work begins on the bus station in the early 1980s.

Storm clouds herald a difficult time for the early days of the Pyramid situated at the side of the M60. Original plans were for a 'King's valley' of Pyramids, but only one was eventually built. Co-operative Bank is now resident in the building.

A photograph of the four stages of a Lunar eclipse was digitally added to this view of the Pyramid for dramatic effect. Used in colour on the front page of the *Stockport Express* it proved very popular with readers who requested dozens of reprints, January 2001.

These were the final dramatic seconds in the life of the 109-year-old Lancashire Hill Mill, demolished in April 1989 by Fred Dibnah. Permission was refused to use explosives, so Fred used his traditional 'pit prop and bonfire' method. Picture taken using a motor-drive camera and then a montage of the sequence was completed.

'Did you like that?' – television personality steeplejack Fred Dibnah repeats his trademark phrase, after felling the Lancashire Hill Mill chimney (above).

Construction of what is now part of the Manchester M60 ring road. This picture was taken in the early 1980s. Note the Pyramid (bottom right) is yet to be built.

Bents Lane, Bredbury. This picture was taken during 1980 with the help of a local pilot as a series for the *Stockport Express*. Bents Lane is from top left to bottom right on the picture. All the industry associated with Bredbury Steel works has long since been replaced with housing estates.

Stockport power station from the air in the early 1980s. This site has been developed out of all recognition – Newbridge Lane can be seen running bottom left to right and the old Burrell factory is now a supermarket. Industrial units now line the right of Newbridge Lane which is just grass on this picture.

Early 1980s photograph of Stockport centre. The power station has long since gone making way for the Peel Centre. Can you spot the changes to our town since then?

Compstall Village looking over Etherow valley, a favourite place for visitors to the Country Park. Photograph taken from the air in 1980. Mill chimney (centre right) has now been demolished.

Not exactly Walt Disney productions – Ritz Cinema (now demolished), December 1982.

Merseyway in the early 1980s. Motorway construction is just starting (top right), Sainsbury's supermarket is yet to be built (bottom right) and facing what is now ASDA supermarket (bottom left).

Apart from the shop signs, 24 years have seen little change on Petersgate, as can be seen from our picture taken in 1978.

Perhaps many older drinkers remember their local Club House pub on Didsbury Road. Demolished for the motorway development. This picture was taken in 1977.

Hardly a Boddington's brewery flagship but this small pub, the Huntsman's Tavern, had many local devotees. This photograph was taken beside the cobbled Huntsman Brow in 1977.

Egerton Arms prior to demolition in the late 1970s. This pub was on Brinksway Road and nicknamed 'The Crackers' by locals. It gained this name because of the Chesters beer sold which had a reputation as 'fighting beer' – a description that is self explanatory!

Located on the junction of Georges Road and Heaton Lane, the Gardener's Arms is now just a memory after many years of dispensing Robinson's beer.

Demolition of the North West Water building, St Petersgate, in April 1997.

Another familiar building that is no longer with us. Stockport swimming baths, or Petersgate Recreation Centre to give it a 'Sunday title', pictured in November 1989.

Wellington boots, a hard hat – and possibly a peg on the end of his nose – were essential garb for the staff photographer who took this picture in new sewers under Didsbury Road during 1976.

Remember the rag and bone man? John Broad & Son were one of last to send horses and carts on to Stockport's streets. Pictured during April 1976 is one of their many carts ready to collect rags and scrap metal from householders.

This particular rag and bone cart became a casualty of modern traffic after a collision with a car in Mersey Square in August 1977.

The Poco A Poco night club and casino, Heaton Chapel. This was a popular evening venue for many years. A serious fire in 1986, after it was renamed Chesters, led to its demolition in 1987.

Demolition cranes make short work of the Poco A Poco in 1987.

Gone but not forgotten – Davenport Theatre is looking a little ragged at the edges in this picture taken in the early 1980s.

Demolition of the Burrell Colours site on Newbridge Lane was completed with this dramatic felling of the factory chimney.

Last days for the Davenport Theatre as demolition work starts in 1987.

Frederic Robinson started brewing beer at the rear of the Unicorn public house in 1860. Now a leading regional brewery, traditional wooden barrels were made by their craftsmen, until the early 1990s began their gradual replacement with aluminium ones.

Robinson's brewery chairman Peter Robinson (right) together with Margaret Thatcher, during her visit to the Unicorn Brewery, June 1983.

Christy and Co Ltd's hat works in 1997. Founded in London in 1773, and moving to Stockport in 1826, the company closed on Hillgate with the loss of 111 jobs in 1998. One of the more colourful orders was for an African chief who required pink top hats. These were manufactured in the normal way and then painted with Dulux emulsion paint!

Brian Johnson visits Christy's hat works for BBC radio's *Down Your Way*. Helping Brian choose a hat is managing director Mr Jack Wallworth, in our picture from the early 1980s.

Hats off to history – machinists Marlene Evans of Reddish (served 44 years) and Audrey Russell of Offerton (served 35 years) during the last year of Christy hat production in 1997.

'Hello, hello.' Raymond Rowe retires after 50 years at Christy's hat works in 1986. During his time he was responsible for the production of more than half a million items of police headwear.

A top machinist for a top hat. Mrs Jean Griffiths finishes the hats by putting a white band on them. A scene gone forever at Christy & Co Ltd.

Hot work for Jimmy Handrahan of Reddish, as he completes a process that had hardly changed for hundreds of years. This photograph was taken during the last year of production in 1997.

45596 *Bahamas* in less glamorous days than the accompanying picture. Here she is stuck, hemmed in by a less illustrious fellow locomotive, behind Edgeley Park football ground.

Driver Jack Moores of Cheadle Hulme, proudly points to the *Stopfordian* train nameplate given for the day to the famous steam locomotive *Bahamas*, Edgeley Station, 23 September 1991.

Winter wonderland: Peter Wright from Avondale School uses a heavy snowfall for skiing practice in Hollywood Park in December 1981.

Remember the hard winters? Snow drifts on the side roads towards Rowarth above Marple Bridge in February 1981.

Work just starting during 1979 on what is now the M60 Manchester Ring Road. Bulldozers slice a path through the red sandstone with St Mary's RC Church (top left) and Merseyway Precinct to the right.

Moving a mountain – almost. Another view of the motorway construction during 1979 as bulldozers move thousands of tons of sandstone from what is now a vertical cutting from St Mary's Church down to the motorway.

Looking towards the viaduct with Merseyway on the left, is this view of groundwork starting on the motorway in 1981.

Empty apart from a solitary worker, as the motorway (now the the M60) nears completion in 1982.

A technological revolution in the printing industry forced the last revolution of this metal plate-making machine at the *Stockport Express* during 1982. Proving he had a 'hands-on' approach to business, is Mr Ernest Petrie who was managing director during this period.

Last of the hot metal printers at the *Stockport Express*. Many of these faces took redundancy during the transition to computerised production in 1991.

Chadkirk Dyeworks, next to the canal, is pictured in our photograph from February 1978.

Flood waters of the River Goyt rage underneath Otterspool Bridge, Romiley, winter 2000.

Lyme Park 'cage' after restoration in April 1999.

Hard News

Dramatic picture minutes after a British Midland Argonaut DC4 aircraft crashed into Hopes Carr, near the centre of Stockport, on the Sunday morning of 4 June 1967.

A special edition of the *Stockport Express* published a day after the tragic accident in June 1967.

The British Midland DC-4 Argonaut airliner that crashed near the centre of Stockport on the morning of 4 June 1967. Fuel problems caused the aircraft to lose power on the final approach to Manchester Airport. An even worse disaster was avoided by the pilot managing to avoid nearby tower blocks of flats and crash landing into Hopes Carr – the only area of open land in this heavily built-up area.

Spectators were inexorably drawn to the crash site of the British Midland Argonaut.

Tail unit of the Argonaut aircraft with the 'BM' initials of British Midland faintly showing after fire gutted the aircraft that crashed into Hopes Carr near the centre of Stockport, June 1967.

Gangland boss Chris Little with one of his beloved Staffordshire bull terriers. Chris Little was 31 when he was shot through the head with a 12-bore shotgun from another car, as he stopped his black Mercedes at traffic lights in Marple in 1994.

Chris Little's £50,000 Mercedes. He was killed instantly at the wheel of the car which ploughed into two vehicles, before crashing into the wall of the Bowling Green pub, Marple.

Utter despair for investors, during the Barlow Clowes financial scandal in 1988. Thousands of investors lost life savings when the Barlow Clowes Investment Group folded in a £190 million crash. Peter Clowes started a business in Heaton Moor selling paraffin from the back of a van. He was found guilty of stealing £17 million and was jailed in 1992 after a seven-month trial.

Double killer Robert Healey arrives at Stockport Magistrates Court. Jailed for life in April 1987, he was convicted of the murder of his wife, Greeba, and 13-year-old stepdaughter, Marie. Reggie Perrin fan Healey tried to avoid arrest by faking his own suicide with a Perrin-style plot by leaving his clothes on a Prestatyn beach, but eventually gave himself up.

Double killer Robert Healey leaves Stockport Magistrates Court.

Police take away a demonstrator during anti poll-tax demonstrations outside Stockport Town Hall in 1990.

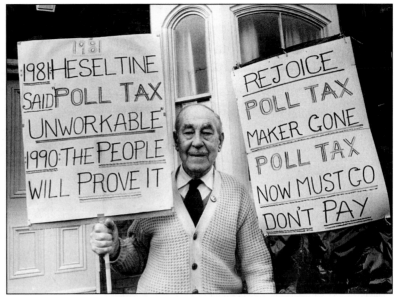

Poll Tax objector Frank Taylor from Heaton Chapel was very active locally and appeared on our pages a number of times.

Local pilot Barry Bryant had an incredible escape in 1983 when his Cessna 150 crashed into the side of Kinder Scout near Edale in bad weather. Barry and his passenger escaped serious injury and walked down the mountain to the Nag's Head at Edale and told the landlord, 'We have parked our vehicle a little further away than most of your customers!' Barry is now a training captain flying the Regional Jet with BaE systems.

Reaching the summit of Everest in 1975, Peter Boardman was renowned as one of the world's greatest climbers. This picture was taken in his New Mills home in January 1982. Several months later he lost his life, together with Joe Tasker, as they attempted the North East Ridge of Everest without oxygen. Chris Bonington was also on this ill-fated attempt to climb the world's highest and most unforgiving mountain.

British Airtours Boeing 737 *River Orrin* with passenger chutes and flight deck escape webbing deployed. Fifty-four people died from a total of 139 passengers and crew when an engine explosion ignited fuel during take-off at Manchester Airport in August 1985.

Margaret Thatcher visits the British Airtours Boeing 737 crash site at Manchester Airport, August 1985.

A senior police officer gives an early morning briefing to members of the press in the aftermath of the Manchester Airport disaster.

British Airtours Boeing 737 disaster, August 1985. An explosion in the port engine ignited fuel as flight KT328 was on its 7am take off for Corfu.

Nicholas Geldard (10) died from a brain haemorrhage after a brain scan was refused at Stepping Hill Hospital. He was desperately shunted between four hospitals and a lack of intensive-care beds culminated in a 2am dash across the Pennines to Leeds – but Nicholas was found brain dead on arrival. Pictured with members of the Geldard family are people signing a petition directed at the Secretary of State for Health.

The day WE made the news – Peter Greenwood, then our editor-in-chief, is interviewed by *Panorama* for the Nicholas Geldhart story in 1996. This programme was shown worldwide after our hard-hitting story blamed the NHS for Nicholas's death.

Cannabis campaigner Colin Davies is arrested in September 2001. Owner of the Dutch Experience café in Stockport, Mr Davies, founder of the controversial Medical Marijuana Co-operative, had presented The Queen with a 'bouquet' of cannabis plants, during her visit to the Lowry Centre the previous year.

David Barnshaw murder press conference at Stockport police headquarters in 1999.

Forensic detectives inspect the Ford Orion car where David Barnshaw was found burnt to death in 1999. This horrific crime was described by a senior police officer as 'the worst I have known in 28 years service'.

Chestergate Auto Centre murders – police check for clues in November 1993. MoT inspectors Alan Singleton and Simon Bruno were both shot dead at point-blank range with a shotgun. Garage owner Thomas Bourke, who disguised himself with a Halloween mask for the killing, was jailed for life in December 1994.

Chestergate Auto Centre murders – a police press conference reports progress at the time of the horrific double murder in November 1993.

Guns on the streets – an armed robbery in Disley led to an intensive search of the streets of Offerton, after the criminals were traced to that area in April 1999.

Surrounded by curious youngsters, armed police would have a difficult responsibility if their guns were needed during a search for armed criminals, after a robbery in Disley in April 1999.

Car graveyard off Birdhall Lane. These cars were stolen, destroyed and dumped on waste ground. This picture was used during December 1999 to illustrate endemic car theft and vandalism in Stockport.

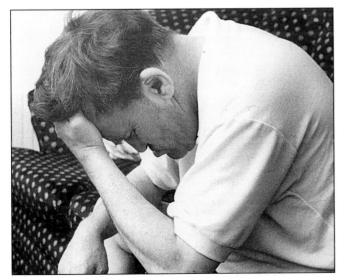

'Care in the Community' – a strong image that was used on the front page for a hard hitting report called the 'Outsiders'. This picture was a major contribution to the *Express Advertiser* becoming the *UK Press Gazette's* Weekly Newspaper of the Year in 1992. Pictured is Donald Turner who wanted to return to Offerton House where he had lived for more than 30 years.

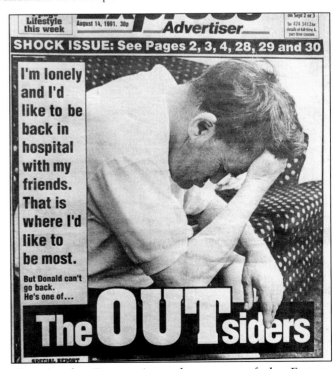

Care in the Community – front page of the *Express Advertiser* in August 1991.

A bitter struggle during the two-year Roberts Arundel industrial dispute from 1966 until 1968. All 145 employees were sacked by the new American owner after he illegally employed cheap labour. Police threatened AEU officials with the Riot Act – an extreme measure which entitles police to shoot and kill if a crowd does not disperse. Fortunately against a background of large press coverage this was not evoked. *Stockport Express* photographers attended throughout the dispute.

A 7am arrival of 'scab' non-union workers in September 1967 is met by strikers during the bitter Roberts Arundel industrial dispute.

Concerned looks from shop stewards during a march through Stockport in support of striking Roberts Arundel workers in 1967.

A protester is led away by police during the Roberts Arundel dispute.

Confrontation ends with arrest for one of the protesters at Roberts Arundel.

Police and workers confront each other during the 1967 Roberts Arundel dispute.

The Stockport
mayoral car
faces a gauntlet
of angry
demonstrators
supporting
sacked Roberts
Arundel
workers.

Roberts Arundel marchers, 1967.

More strikers on the march.

An anti-National Front demonstrator is dragged away by police, during a 1978 march by the National Front from Levenshulme to Stockport. Union flags used as a standard by the National Front can be seen in the background.

Anti-National Front demonstrators march through lines of police during a NF rally in 1978.

Police, including one Asian officer, separate National Front members from opposing factions as they march past Stockport Town Hall in 1985.

Mounted police were called up when a National Front march brought disorder to Stockport in 1985.

A bomb disposal expert prepares a remote control crawler to investigate a possible explosive device in Edgeley in 1992. The 'bomb' was a false alarm, but gave the soldier – and photographer – a few anxious moments.

OFFICIAL PICKET

SOUND YOUR HORN & SUPPORT YOUR FIREMEN

A determined stance during the 1977 firemen's strike. These pickets were outside King Street West fire headquarters.

An RAF fire tender responds to a fire at C & A, Merseyway, during the firemen's strike of 1977.
Note the price on the menu board in the foreground – chips and beefburger, 24p!

A fireman's lift for a soldier overcome by smoke during a fire at the Nield & Hardy music store on Chestergate, Great Underbank, in December 1977. Soldiers took the place of striking firemen.

During the 1977 firemen's strike, a senior fire officer surveys the roof of the timbered National Westminster Bank building as fire raged in the nearby Nield & Hardy music store. Fortunately the fire did not spread to this old and vunerable building.

Soldiers taking the place of striking regular firemen struggle to contain a fire that gutted Nield & Hardy's store at Great Underbank in December 1977.

Fire! A blaze at a Brinksway used tyre company is tackled by firemen in 1980.

Hope Mills, Portwood, destroyed by fire in October 1998.

During July 1983, six printers at the Stockport office of the *Messenger* group of newspapers went on strike after a dispute with the owner, Eddie Shah. This small dispute led eventually to mass pickets by thousands of print union members at the newspaper's plant in Warrington. Our picture, taken during November 1983, shows a violent confrontation between police and pickets.

Print workers and journalists from the *Stockport Messenger* picket the Stockport offices at the start of the dispute in July 1983.

Storm damage – a tree fell on a car in Chester Road, Hazel Grove, in 1984.

Pictures Royal

The Queen Mother arrives at Stockport Town Hall in an open-topped car at the start of her visit in June 1960.

The Queen Mother's arrival at Stockport Town Hall in 1960.

The Queen Mother waves to the crowd at Stockport Town Hall in 1960.

Crowds wait outside the Infirmary for the arrival of the Queen Mother in 1960.

The Queen Mother, together with Mayor of Stockport, Councillor Clara Grant, and Colonel John Christie-Miller, during her visit to the Christie hat factory, June 1960.

Christie's hat factory employees await the arrival of the Queen Mother.

The Queen Mother inspects Royal Marines cadets at St Anne's Hospice.

No luxury of several-frames-a-second photography for this 1960 photographer as he struggles with a heavy camera and pocketful of glass plates.

Her Majesty The Queen drives past the old *Stockport Express* building on St Peter's Square in 1968. It was rumoured that the best china cups and a fresh pot of tea was ready just in case she decided to visit!

Princess Margaret visits Romiley Forum in 1972.

Local press photographers from the *Stockport Express*, *Stockport Advertiser*, and *Manchester Evening News* await the arrival of Princess Margaret, Romiley Forum, 1972.

'One prefers the Royal Yacht.' The Duke of Edinburgh shares a joke with Sea Cadets during his visit to Pendlebury Hall, Stockport, in May 1972.

The Duke of Edinburgh on his visit to Pendlebury Hall in May 1972.

Prince Charles on board the *New Horizons*, a specially adapted canal cruiser for wheelchair users, at Marple Locks in 1981. Prince Charles took part in the official naming ceremony of the boat which was the brainchild of the Mayor of Stockport, Councillor Gordon Bayley (pictured left).

Her Majesty The Queen, together with Mayor of Stockport, Councillor Basil Thompson, during her visit to Edgeley Park football ground for the 1977 jubilee celebrations.

Her Majesty The Queen visits Edgeley Park in 1977, her silver jubilee year.

Still got the tee-shirt? These youngsters enjoying the 1977 silver jubilee celebrations will almost certainly have children of their own by now.

A silver jubilee street party at Alberta Street, Hillgate.

Time for a 'knees-up' at the Greg Street silver jubilee party in 1977.

Residents of Greg Street enjoy their silver jubilee street party in 1977.

This time it is the turn of Marsden Avenue, Romiley, to celebrate the 1977 silver jubilee.

Waiting to tuck in at the Alderley Drive, Romiley, street party.

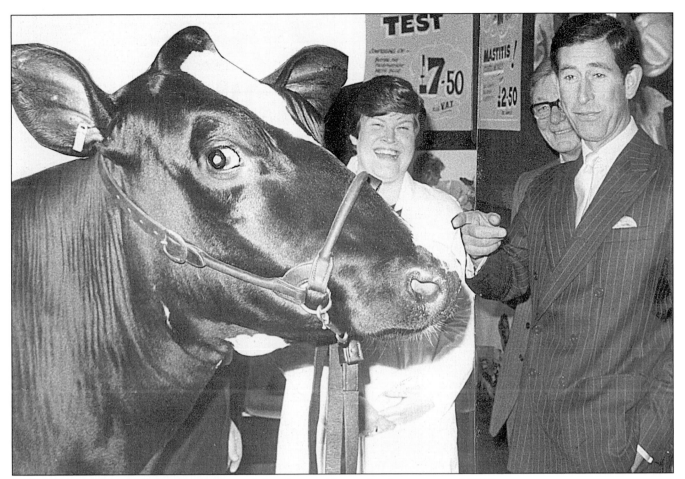

'Who's that with Daisy?' Prince Charles at Manchester Airport in the autumn of 1986.

Prince Charles chats to the locals during his visit to Houldsworth Mill, Reddish, in 1997.

The Princess Royal riding *Black Ice* over the water jump during the Lyme Park Horse trials in September 1987.

A 'Royal Special' front page, after the Queen's visit to Stockport in March 1991.

An attack of nerves for four-year-old Amy-Jayne Hodgkinson when she refused to present Princess Anne with a bouquet of flowers during the opening of Manchester Airport Rail Link. *Stockport Express and Times* picture editor Chris Hill received a 'highly commended' award for this picture at the Fuji European Press Photographer of the Year awards in 1993.

Diana, Princess of Wales, visits Didsbury in March 1993.

'But they are for YOU!' Princess Diana confused this young gentleman when she returned a single rose for him, after he presented her with a posie at St Anne's Hospice, Heald Green, in October 1985.

On her 1985 visit, Princess Diana illustrated that special rapport she had with the public.

Princess Diana meets her fans at St Anne's Hospice.

IN MEMORY OF

DIANA, PRINCESS OF WALES

STOCKPORT MARKET WILL BE CLOSED

ON

SATURDAY, 6 SEPTEMBER 1997

Along with the rest of the nation, the citizens of Stockport were stunned by the tragic death of Princess Diana.

Princess Anne visiting Marple in May 1996.

Princess Anne at Hazel Grove in May 1994.

The Queen and Prince Philip arrive at Edgeley Station in October 2000.

A royal smile for the crowds at Edgeley Station after local dignitaries were presented to The Queen.

The Queen shares a joke with Anne Coffey MP.

Her Majesty The Queen leaves Stockport Station for a visit to Manchester in October 2000.

The Duke of Edinburgh visits the Co-operative Bank offices in the Pyramid Building in 2000.

Queen look-alike Elizabeth Richards was the nearest Stockport came to a 'royal' visit during the Golden Jubilee celebrations. Tanya Forrest (four) of Heaton Norris is pictured with 'Her Majesty' at the Stockport Hat Museum in June 2002.

Politicians in Focus

A 'big gun' in the shape of David Lloyd George was brought to Stockport to support the Liberal candidate in a 1925 by-election. Prime Minister during World War One, Lloyd George (centre) is pictured here outside the Heaton Reform Club.

Enoch Powell speaks to a packed house at the Alma Lodge Hotel. This was about the period of his famous 'Rivers of Blood' speech, an extreme warning on the dangers of racial disharmony.

Liberal leader Jeremy Thorpe, during a meeting at Bramhall High School in March 1976.

Harold Wilson in classic pose together with Andrew Bennett MP (left) and former Greater Manchester Council leader Bernard Clarke, during a visit to Cheadle Heath Primary School.

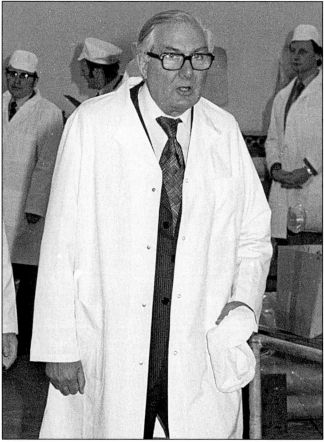

Looking lost – James Callaghan during a visit to McVitie's in the 1970s.

A crumpled suit and a firm handshake were the order of the day for politicians in 1970. George Brown chats with this lady in Merseyway precinct. She looks as if she will 'handbag' him if he says anything that she disagrees with.

Relaxing with a beer – Ted Heath in the White Hart, Cheadle, with Tom Normanton MP, in 1970.

A cold wind blows for Roy Hattersley in March 1979 as he visits Adamson Containers, Reddish. A cold wind also blew for the company during February of that year, as a lorry drivers' strike forced the company to cut production by 50 per cent.

Roy Hattersley is shown a model of how R. Greg & Co Ltd, Reddish, was to be modernised, March 1979. During 1982 the Albert Mill on Greg Street closed for the manufacture of textiles after 136 years.

Roy Hattersley with three-year-old Liam Hart in the Merseyway precinct.

Local model Michelle Hall stole the picture when she met MPs Leon Britton and Tony Favell on a walkabout in Castle Street in the 1980s.

Michael Heseltine makes his point as Hazel Grove MP Tom Arnold listens intently.

One of the lads – Liberal leader David Steel seems to have made some friends during his visit to Marple Liberal Club in 1985.

Margaret Thatcher with the candidate for Stockport North during a visit to Castle Street before the 1979 General Election.

The small child in the foreground is more interested in the photographer than Margaret Thatcher in Castle Street.

On the election trail – Margaret Thatcher and Tom Arnold MP.

'Smile for the photographer' – Margaret Thatcher prompts JEL employee Sue Carroll during a visit to the Hazel Grove factory in 1987.

One for the road – John Major stops for a pint on the election trail, during a visit to Governors House pub, Cheadle Hulme, in May 2001.

A classic shoulder-shaking laugh from Edward Heath during a visit to Stockport in 1986. Mr Heath is pictured with Tom Arnold MP. We are uncertain who the baby is perched on Mr Arnold's shoulder!

Labour leader Neil Kinnock (centre) during a visit to Stockport in 1983. Andrew Bennett MP is pictured left.

Andrew Bennett MP and Anne Coffey hand over a 'Stockport Infirmary Opt-Out' petition to Glenys Kinnock (second left) and Harriet Harman (centre) at Manchester Airport in March 1992.

Chief Superintendent Paul Cook shows Michael Howard (the then Conservative Home Secretary) around an exhibition for Operation Jigsaw promoting drugs awareness and education.

Official Monster Raving Loony party candidate Colin Hewitt gets his message across during the 1997 General Election.

Tea and chat for Kenneth Baker (then chairman of the Conservative Party), during a visit to Cheadle Hulme Conservative Club.

Sir Geoffrey Howe at Heaton Mersey Conservative Club during the 1983 General Election campaign.

Handshakes win more friends than right-hooks – John Prescott in benign mood as he greets Cheadle Labour Club secretary Paul Lee. Also pictured is Jack Straw (left) and Mr George Howarth at the start of a political meeting at the club, June 1992.

Famous Faces

Obviously making an impression – Mike Yarwood who was Stockport County's honorary vice-president for several years, clowns for the camera in September 1976. Mike was arguably one of the country's best impersonators during the 1960-70s. Born in Stockport in 1941, he became an ardent Hatters fan.

'Take One' – Stockport Market becomes a film set for an episode of *Coronation Street* as Vera Duckworth (Elizabeth Dawn) and Elsie Tanner (Pat Phoenix) spin their magic for a 'soap' that has been exported to television sets all over the world.

Peter Sellers filming *The Pink Panther* at Manchester Airport in June 1976.

'Elementary my dear Watson – we are to appear in the *Stockport Express*.' Sherlock Holmes (Jeremy Brett) seems to explain the plot to a baffled Dr Watson (Edward Hardwicke), during filming for a Granada series of *Sherlock Holmes* at Lyme Hall in 1984.

Rosemary Conley (centre), author of *The Hip and Thigh Diet*, pictured at Heald Green Public Hall in 1994.

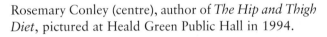

Remember Billy Two Rivers? He was a popular contestant on the all-in wrestling circuit during the 1960s and '70s. A full-bloodied Native American, he was actively involved in campaigns for Indian civil rights. Billy (left) is pictured during a visit to the Old King pub on Portwood, together with licensee Steve Haggerty, in 1982.

The pop group Mud at Bredbury Hall, riding the world's smallest motorcycles – which they carried around in a Cadillac in July 1976. Mud recorded recorded hits such as *Tiger Feet*.

Coronation Street's Len Fairclough (Peter Adamson) signs autographs, during a visit to the Rediffusion shop on Merseyway in 1976.

Phil Cool pulls one of his faces during a book signing in the early 1980s.

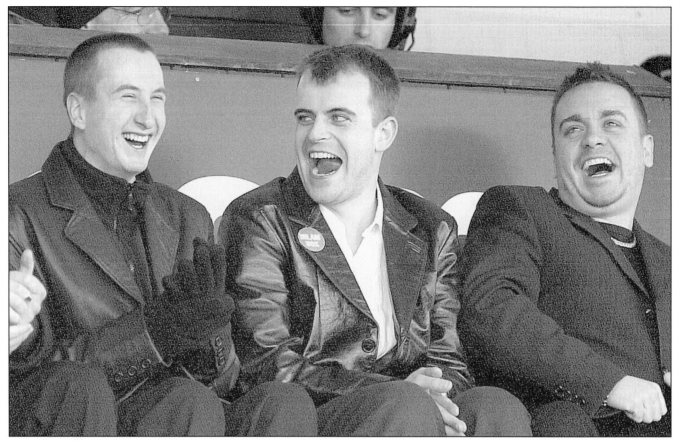

Debating a Stockport County win perhaps? *Coronation Street* stars visit Edgeley Park to watch the Stockport County v Wolves match in February 2002. Pictured (from the left) are Kirk Sutherland (Andrew Whyment), Steve McDonald (Simon Gregson) and Jez Quigley (Lee Boardman).

Antiques Roadshow personality David Battie gives his expert opinion on a teapot, during a filming of the ever-popular BBC programme at Lyme Hall in June 1988.

Julie Hesmondhalgh who plays Hayley Cropper in *Coronation Street*, opens the DEBRA charity shop at Romiley in May 1999.

Bernard Manning referees a celebrity football match at the Jewish Primary School, Heald Green in 1993. He is pictured showing a red card to Nick Conway (left) and former Manchester City star Frank Carrodus (right). Highgrove captain Chris Clark is in the centre.

We are here – Emily Walker (eight), a Larkhill Primary School pupil, holds up the Universe for Patrick Moore as he opens the Stockport Binocular and Telescope Centre's science room in September 1997.

Bruce Jones (*Coronation Street's* Les Battersby) celebrates with a cuppa after opening the Mallard Tea Room at Compstall in June 2001.

A classic clown pose from Norman Wisdom during a visit to Barton Grange Garden Centre, Woodford, in 1997. Norman is a superb subject for any photographer, a consummate professional, polite, natural and genuinely funny. Norman has appeared many times in our pages throughout the years.

An episode of *Neighbours* was filmed in Lyme Park in the late 1980s. Together with Madge and Harold (Anne Charleston and Ian Smith) is Derek Nimmo (left). Apparently the Australian stars had come to Lyme to find their roots and Derek's character was there to greet them in the episode.

You needed a little more than a 'tickling-stick' to rent the Pyramid in its early days. Ken Dodd tried his best and perhaps he worked his magic, because the Co-operative Bank seems a happy resident at the moment.

Ken Dodd repels borders (in a half-hearted fashion) as these young ladies try to board the *New Horizons* canal narrow boat at Marple. This boat has been specially adapted for the disabled and has given much pleasure to many people over many years – just like Ken Dodd!

Geoffrey Hughes, well-known to TV viewers for his work in *Heartbeat* and *The Royle Family*, was at the Brookside Railway, Poynton, in December 1996 with the Roly Polys and the rest of the cast of the pantomime *Aladdin*.

Ian Botham, Max Boyce and other members of the cast of the pantomime *Jack and the Beanstalk* at the Davenport Theatre in the 1992–3 season.

Plaza Theatre photo call for *Cinderella* starring Martin Hancock (left) as Buttons and Kathy Staff as the Fairy Godmother.

Wolf from *Gladiators*, Jimmy Saville and Max Boyce switch on the Christmas lights at Merseyway precinct in1992.

The late – and great – Les Dawson in fine form together with the Roly Polys in 1996.

Lynne Perrie (Ivy Tisley from *Coronation Street*) and Mother Goose outside the Davenport Theatre in 1994.

Sue Pollard opens Eye Sight, a local opticians in Stockport in the 1980s.

Manchester United's Andy Cole attends Stockport magistrates court for a driving offence in 1999.

Sir Bernard Lovell, who designed the Jodrell Bank radio telescope, pictured together with Revd Amos Cresswell, prior to a service at Cheadle Hulme Methodist Church in May 1969.

Neil and Christine Hamilton record their 2001 Christmas Day radio show, with the help of Christine's cuddly gorilla Eric at the Heaton Lane studios of Imagine FM.

Groundforce star Charlie Dimmock together with Stockport Deputy Mayor Michael Wilson (left) and a new plant called Golden Russian Vine presented by David Andrews (right), during her visit to Barton Grange Garden Centre in 1999.

Aladdin panto star Toyah Wilcox poses for a fire safety promotion during December 2001. A 999 call left Toyah without her supporting cast of firemen as they dashed off, complete with 'Welliphant', in response to an emergency.

Aviation in Stockport

One of the first aircraft to land in Stockport. German flyer Gustav Hamill gave the residents of Adswood a flying display of aerobatics and landed near Bakery Bridge in 1913. Gustav is seen holding the wing (behind the man in the suit). He was killed when his aircraft crashed into the English Channel when returning to Germany just before the outbreak of World War One.

'Professor' Baldwin's balloon makes an ascent from Cale Green in 1892, filled with gas from the local gas main. He ascended hanging from a sling underneath with a parachute already deployed (bottom left of balloon). Jumping from the balloon he landed in Hall Street and dislocated his arm. He is reported to have been taken to the Blossoms Hotel for some 'thirst' aid.

A beautifully restored vintage Avro 504K flys over Woodford. Note the wording 'A.V. Roe & Co Ltd, Manchester', on the fuselage. This famous biplane was used to train RAF pilots.

'Look no hands' – the pilot gives a wave from another Avro product, an Avro Tutor trainer, at Woodford Airshow in 1995.

Fairey Aviation was an important part of industrial Stockport during World War Two. Our picture shows a pair of superbly restored Fairey Swordfish, aptly nicknamed 'Stringbags', ready to roll, prior to their display during the 1983 Woodford Airshow. Some of the manufacture of this type of aircraft was completed in Heaton Chapel.

A restored Fairey Firefly flys over Woodford in 1994. Like the Swordfish, some models of this aircraft were constructed or converted at Fairey's Heaton Chapel works. They were then transported by road to Ringway for flight testing.

End of a valiant flying career for Wing Commander David Penman DSO, OBE, DFC, seated in the front cockpit of this World War Two vintage De Havilland Tiger Moth. Wing Commander Penman lived in Stockport for many years and was an Avro Lancaster bomber pilot, earning his DSO for a daylight raid on a vital U-boat engine factory in Augsburg, Germany. His aircraft, *U-Uncle*, was one of the few to return. This staff picture was taken in 1977 to mark his retirement from flying training aircraft with the RAFVR (Volunteer Reserve).

British Aerospace chief test pilot Peter Henley with Algy, his unofficial Labrador co-pilot. Algy, named after fictional hero Biggle's sidekick Algernon, joined his master on many flights strapped into the cockpit. The original caption for this picture in 1992 suggested he was set for a 'dog-fight' – such are journalistic puns!

Woodford Airshow – an Avro Lancaster prepares for take off. Woodford assembly lines worked day and night during World War Two to keep ahead of the dreadful rate of bombers lost in action.

A Lancaster of the RAF Memorial Flight on its approach to Woodford for the 1991 airshow.

Woodford Airshow – Former BAE fitter Allan Crosthwaite of Mellor, in an Avro Anson 19. The aircraft has been restored by the Avro Heritage Society formed by retired BAE employees.

Woodford Airshow – Nearing completion after its Woodford restoration, the 1946 Avro Anson. Pictured at the controls are the project co-ordinator Derrick Bowyer and former Woodford fitter Allan Crosthwaite (of Mellor), both members of the Avro Heritage Society (formed by retired BAE employees) 1996.

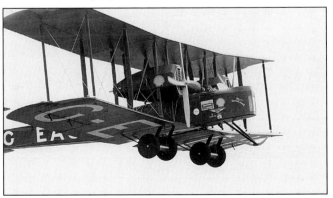

Woodford Airshow, 1996 – a replica of a Vickers Vimy.

Woodford Airshow – 'The Last of the Many'; Spitfire, Hurricane and Lancaster all prepare to take-off.

Spitfire pilot David Moore taxis a Rolls-Royce-powered Mk14 Spitfire just prior to his fatal crash at Woodford Airshow in June 1992.

Spitfire pilot David Moore flys over the emergency services vehicles that moments later rushed in vain to his aid after he crashed on the runway.

Vulcan XM603 in squadron service. in the late 1970s. This aircraft is the last Vulcan at Woodford, and sits on the airfield painted in white anti-flash paint, a colour used for its original role to drop an atomic warhead from high altitude. Ending its operational career in 1982, it was stripped of parts to keep other Vulcans flying during the Falklands war. During its service it ranged far and wide including Canada, USA and New Zealand.

The pilot of a Japanese World War two Zeke Zero aircraft at the 1991 Woodford Airshow.

This Avro Vulcan bomber rattles the window panes as full throttle is applied for take-off at Woodford. This local product was never used in anger until the very end of its service life, against Argentinian targets during the Falklands war.

Last of the Vulcans – four of these aircraft make a last farewell to their birthplace, as they fly over Woodford for the last time in April 1984. Designed to be part of the UK nuclear deterrent they only saw action during the 1982 Falklands war when two Vulcans flew 3,900 miles from Ascension Island to bomb Port Stanley runway.

Old and the new, in 1980, at Woodford, a Shackleton flies over a Nimrod which was to replace the 30-year-old piston-engined design.

Crew of the last airborne early warning Shackleton aircraft to fly into Woodford in 1991. Produced at the Woodford factory, these aircraft gave over 40 years of service to the RAF.

One of the last flights over Woodford for the AEW Shackleton prior to its final retirement in 1991.

The largest variant of the BAE 125 – the '1,000' version – pictured in 1991.

Nimrod taking off at Woodford Airshow.

BAe Nimrod MR2 sub-hunter at Woodford Airshow in June 1991. A current nine-year order to refurbish these aircraft has brought much needed work to the Woodford factory.

Airborne early-warning Nimrod roll-out 1980. A Woodford project that was beset with problems.

Remember Dan-Air, a defunct airline that flew many Stockport people to package tour destinations? This particular aircraft was one of the first Avro 748 aircraft to be built and had just taken enthusiasts on its last passenger-carrying flight for Dan-Air, becoming just too old to operate economically. Pictured third right in the group of people in 1980 is air historian Brian Robinson, who lived Stockport and, alas, died recently.

BA test pilot Charles Masefield demonstrates the low level single-engined performance of the 748-2B in 1980.

Test pilots Charles Masefield of Prestbury and Bob Dixon-Stubbs of Bramhall, during the first passenger-carrying flight of the 748-2B. Bob Dixon-Stubbs was a member of the crew on the 748 prototype 20 years before this picture was taken in 1980

A BAe multi-role 748 demonstrator was a home-grown participant at the Woodford Airshow in the early 1980s.

A Macavia water tanker version of the BAe 748 demonstrates its fire-fighting capability during the Woodford Airshow in the early 1980s.

Air enthusiasts always looked forward to Woodford Airshow, but many years were blessed with typical northern weather as depicted by our picture during the 1997 show.

August 1980 and BAe test pilot Robbie Robinson checks his watch after the ATP's (Advanced Turboprop) first flight. The time and day of the flight had been planned two years earlier and the project was exactly on schedule to the minute.

BAe Advanced Turboprop (ATP) aircraft, a Woodford project that first flew in 1986. Some of the current aircraft are to be converted into a freighter version by a Swedish company.

A Nimrod fuselage is brought to Woodford inside a giant Russian-built Antonov in November 1999.

Another view of this amazing Russian Antonov as a BAe Nimrod is taken from its gigantic cargo hold, Woodford, 1999.

'Top Guns' – Gulf War RAF aircrew use a Tornado as a vantage point to watch the 1991 Woodford Airshow.

Made in Stockport – BAe Avroliner RJ85 owned by Air Malta lands at the Woodford factory in 1995.

Take off at Woodford for the order-winning 146.

A.V. Roe test pilot Jimmy Orrell OBE, pictured with an Avro Anson at Woodford in the early 1980s. Jimmy flight tested over 900 Lancaster bombers from 1942 until 1954, ending his career with the mighty Vulcan. Production of the Anson at Woodford reached a total of 4,703. Patiently posing in the cockpit for our photographer he wistfully suggested that 'I could fly this aircraft now'. But at the age of 81 the thousands of flights in hundreds of different aircraft would have to remain just a fond memory of an incredible career.

Peter Henley, a well-known Woodford test pilot who retired in 1993. He is pictured with a Mosquito, nicknamed the Wooden Warrior because of it bonded ply construction. Mr Henley flew the aircraft during many air displays.

A vintage F86 Sabre at the 1994 Woodford Airshow.

A very rare sight over Woodford. The Beriev Mermaid, Russia's giant amphibious maritime patrol aircraft, makes an appearance at the Woodford Airshow.

The Russians are coming – Woodford airfield became a 'Soviet' base during 1980 as part of a Granada film production. The 'Russian' aircraft is actually a Woodford product – a military version of the Avro 748 painted to look the part.

'Where IS Woodford?' – a member of the RAF free-fall parachute team spots for a location, during an approach to Woodford Airshow in bad weather. *Express* staff photographer was secured with webbing to the side door of the Hercules aircraft for this picture. Picture taken early in the 1980s.

RAF free-fall parachute team

A Harrier vertical take-off and landing jump jet struggles with typical Woodford Airshow weather during the 1997 Airshow.

Military Matters

Cheshire Regiment band. This photograph was taken in France in 1917.

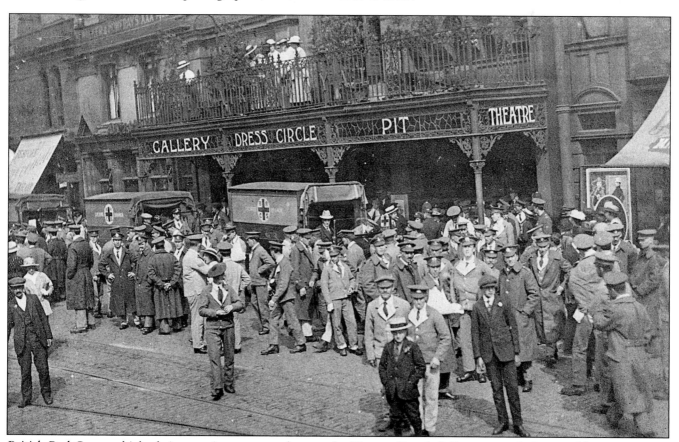

British Red Cross vehicles bring servicemen to a show at the Theatre Royal, St Petersgate, during World War One.

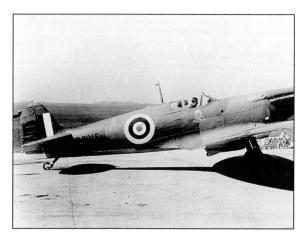

Stockport's own Spitfire. Funds were raised by public donation to purchase this aircraft during the early part of World War Two. Note the name 'Stockport' on the cockpit door.

Front page of the *Stockport Express* Victory Edition. This was produced on 10 May 1945, just after VE day but before the final defeat of the Japanese forces. Despite being one of the one of the most important stories of the 20th century, it still had to compete for space with the small adverts on the front page.

This wartime photograph from our files was captioned: 'Two people were killed when this house suffered a direct hit.' Note the ARP man with his tin helmet and possibly a reporter taking details (left of picture).

Pupils and staff of Banks Lane Junior School celebrate VJ (victory over Japan) Day in August 1945.

The *Last Post* is played by Cheshire Regiment colleagues at the funeral of Lance Corporal Clinton Collins in December 1982. Clinton was among 16 killed and 66 injured by a terrorist bomb attack at the Droppin Well bar, near the Ballykelly headquarters of the Cheshire Regiment, Northern Ireland.

Remembering: For one man personal grief is just too much to bear on Remembrance Day 1988 at the service at Stockport War Memorial.

Ready for battle – TA soldiers based at the Greek Street Armoury are flown to their next offensive position packed into an RAF Chinook helicopter, during a training exercise in Germany in the 1980s.

Local TA soldiers join an exercise in Northern Germany, 1980s

Stockport members of 207 (Manchester) Field Hospital became realistic casualties during an exercise on Gibraltar, May 2001. This staff picture was taken in subterranean defensive positions used by troops on the Rock during World War Two.

Stockport TA soldiers find the hot Cyprus sun tiring as they wait for helicopter deployment, during exercise 'Lion's Pride 2000'.

Stockport members of the Kings and Cheshire Regiment TA winch into a helicopter, during an exercise called 'Lion's Pride' in Cyprus. June 2000

Manchester Airport became a drop zone for Parachute Regiment soldiers, during an Airborne Forces day on 19 October 1988. Local World War Two veterans were invited to witness this mass parachute drop, undoubtedly bringing back many memories of their own dangerous missions.

A gusting wind blew this parachutist into the Manchester Airport fire station building, during the mass air drop. Fortunately his canopy remained inflated and he avoided serious injury, October 1988.

Rapid deployment from a helicopter into a jungle position. Cheshire Regiment, Belize 2000. This picture was taken by staff reporter Kate O'Hara, who joined the Cheshires on this South American exercise.

A local member of the Cheshires discovers exactly what it means to be 'up to his neck in it', as he crosses a deep-running jungle river. Cheshire Regiment on exercise, 2000.

Petty Officer Brian Wright who served on HMS *Active* during the Falklands War is welcomed home by his family at Portwood in 1982.

Michael Meakin of Reddish was given a proud flag-waving welcome, on returning home from the Falklands War in 1982.

A proud moment as Cheshire Regiment soldiers take over guard duties at Buckingham Palace in the early 1980s.

Prince Charles inspects local members of the Cheshire Regiment Association, during the tercentenary celebrations of the Cheshire Regiment. Driving rain did not diminish a proud parade of this historic regiment held on Chester racecourse on 7 July 1989.

A *Stockport Express* reporter and photographer team travelled to Southampton to meet the *Canberra* returning from the Falklands War in July 1982. Amongst the crowds was nine-year-old Rebbeca Bailey from Edgeley, waiting to greet her Royal Marines pen pals. From thousands of troops on the ship our *Stockport Express* duo managed to find them for her!

Nine-year-old Rebbeca Bailey of Edgeley, together with her Royal Marines penfriends, after they had disembarked from the *Canberra* on their return from the Falklands War. Southampton, July 1982.

Ready to roll – Corporal Mike McCamm (26) of Cheadle Hulme, a driver for the commanding officer of the 3rd (Volunteer) Battalion, on a TA exercise in South Wales. Mike joined the Stockport Cadet Force at 18, served with the TA and then joined the regular Cheshire Regiment.

Keeping their heads down under fire – a TA exercise in South Wales in 1998.

Mark Fletcher, who gave the ultimate sacrifice when he jumped from safe cover to help a wounded comrade during the battle of Goose Green during the Falklands War in 1982. Mark, from Edgeley, was 21 when he died alongside 16 other members of the 2nd Battalion Parachute Regiment. A second Stockport soldier, SAS Corporal Michael McHugh, also died when a Sea King helicopter crashed into the South Atlantic.

Sporting Stockport

Stockport County players and officials, 1980–1.

Stockport County players snd officials before the start of the 2000–1 season.

Chris Lawler (left) and Mike Summerbee sign for Stockport County in July 1977. Also pictured is club secretary Terry McCreery (standing left) and manager Alan Thompson.

A pensive Danny Bergara. Uruguayan-born Danny became Stockport County's manager in March 1989. After a disappointing start with County, he took them to the Fourth Division play-offs in 1989–90. Popular with the fans, he steered the team through a successful six years with several visits to Wembley (twice without success for the Autoglass Final). Danny was sacked in March 1995.

Former Manchester United player Lee Sharpe relaxes with the *Stockport Express* at Merseyway Precinct in 1983.

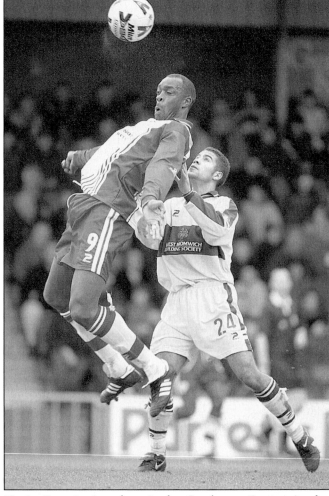

At 6ft 7ins Kevin Francis certainly made his presence felt at Stockport County. Transferred from Derby County, in 1991 for £45,000, he left Edgeley Park in 1995 after scoring 117 goals in 198 matches to join Birmingham City for £800,000.

Kevin Francis signed again for Stockport County in the early part of 2000, staying only for a few months. This picture was taken during the match against West Bromwich Albion at Edgeley Park.

Demolition of the Barlow-Vernon Stand terracing to make way for new seating, Edgeley Park, March 1994.

The new stand under construction at Edgeley Park.

Hats off to the Hatters: Stockport County manager Dave Jones (centre) together with Mike Flynn (top) and Alun Armstrong.

Champagne days for Stockport County after they had beaten Chesterfield 1-0 on 29 April 1997, earning them promotion to the First Division.

Stockport County manager Dave Jones has that 'top of the world' feeling as he greets the thousands who turned up outside Stockport Town Hall to salute him and his promotion-winning club on the Bank Holiday of 5 May 1997.

Stockport County had a disastrous 2001–2 season, ending with relegation after five years in the First Division. Pictured is County's striker Luke Beckett scoring against Bradford City during March 2002. This was the first win of the season after 18 games without a result in their favour.

One of the great personalities of British football – Tommy Docherty. Manager of several clubs including Manchester United, he is currently in great demand as an after-dinner speaker. Tommy is pictured during a visit to Stockport County in 2001.

Mike Flynn, a popular long-serving player (right), pictured during a match against Portsmouth in 2002.

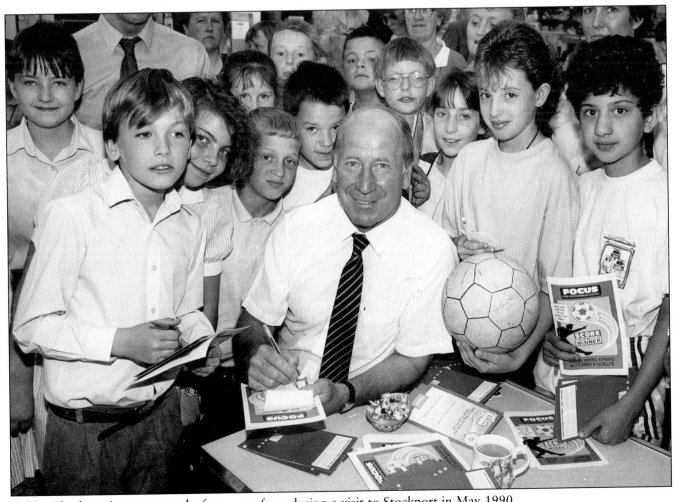

Bobby Charlton signs autographs for young fans, during a visit to Stockport in May 1990.

George Best signs a copy of his book for a delighted fan, Lucia Hall of Hazel Grove, in September 1990.

George Best's former house at Blossoms Lane, Woodford.

Laura Booth (arms raised) joins in the excitement for England's first match during the 1998 World Cup. Co-operative Bank telephone operatives employed in the Pyramid donned shirts and painted faces for the occasion.

The lengths some people will go to for sport. Phil Miller of Reddish paints his car in England colours for the 1998 World Cup.

Like most Northern towns the sport of pigeon racing is serious business in Stockport – perhaps too serious. In 1995, noted fancier Tommy Bradbury lost all his pigeons in an arson attack, but determined to carry on. He won his first race with a new pigeon, aptly named 'Blaze'.

Tom Keene (15) of Heaton Moor was selected for the Junior Cheshire golf squad, during February 2002. A member of Heaton Moor Golf Club, with a handicap of nine, he plays for the men's team, as well as captaining the junior team.

Coming through: Stockport 1st XV v Manchester 2nd XV during a match at Stockport Rugby Club at Headlands Road, Bramhall.

Ruth Maskery, who won the Greater Manchester trampoline championship in 1990.

Disley runner Nick Roberts training on the lush green area near the Moorside Hotel, Disley. Nick was training for a charity marathon taking place in the Sahara Desert. March 2002.

Record-breaking Daniel Dunn (eight) is the youngest Shukokai Karate kid in Britain to gain a black belt. Daniel, of Brinnington, was pictured in February 2002.

Debbie Simms (disabled) and Gerald Price (blind) show off their skills at Sale Water Park in 1989.

A close finish during a sports day for the disabled, held at Avondale Recreation Centre in June 1988.

John Virgo and Paul Medati (right) were regulars in the *Stockport Express Advertiser* snooker handicap, during the 1970s and early 1980s. This picture was taken at the Masters Snooker Centre in 1982. Perhaps they were playing some new rules where both players play the white ball simultaneously – a double trick shot perhaps?

Stockport's tennis legend Fred Perry visits Matchpoint in 1995. Pictured are (from the left) Malcolm Gracie, Richard Parry, Jim Cochrane (chairman of the North-West Sports Council), Fred Perry, and Bob Scott (a member of the Manchester Olympic Committee).

With the exception of the mascot, we wonder how many of these Edgeley Park Rangers team are still playing? Only armchair football no doubt. This picture was taken in 1976, before a match on the New Zealand Road pitches.

Ready for the Sydney Olympics are these Stockport swimmers, Graeme Smith (left) Vicki Horner, Adam Ruckwood and Stephen Parry (right). Photograph taken at Grand Central swimming pool.

Olympic swimmer Andrew Jameson pictured with young swimmers during a Swim Stockport event at Cheadle Baths in March 1989.

Bowling personality Harry Rigby, a Crown Green bowling correspondent for our newspapers for many years. Harry was highly respected both as a character and for his amazing knowledge of the sport.

Good Friday in 1959 was obviously a cold day judging from the overcoats worn by these members of the Victoria Bowling Club. This staff photograph was taken to mark the traditional start of the season for Crown Green bowling – a sport which has been important in Stockport since the 19th century.

Opening of the new pavilion at the Nursery Bowling Club, Heaton Moor, in 1954.

The same scene in 2002. Nursery Bowling Club president Arthur Hibbert opens the season with a veranda added to the pavilion since 1954.

Another season starting for the Victoria Bowling club. President Councillor C. McIndoe bowls the first wood on 20 April 1928. Note that with few exceptions everybody is wearing Stockport's famous product – the hat. It must have been difficult to keep the hats from falling off as they bent down to bowl!

We wonder, how many continue with their training now? Members of Marple Hall cross-country teams prepare for a forthcoming event during the early 1980s.

Going for it – local boxer Jason Roche in training at the new gym opened in the basement of Compstall Library during 1987.

Heaton Norris Amateur Boxing Club at Bredbury Steel Works in February 1976

Boxing champ Chris Eubank together with boxing promoter and owner of the Acton Court Hotel, Jack Trickett. Chris was staying at the hotel, prior to the defence of his WBO title against Paraguayan Carlos Gimenez at the G-MEX Arena, during 1992.

Darts champion Alan Evans (right) pictured with Swedish champion Stefan Lord during a friendly at the Bridgewater Arms in 1977. A previous captain of the Welsh team, Alan moved to Stockport in the early 1970s and became a character in the local darts scene.

Christopher Hancock (10) of Heald Green was one of the few who could do this to strongman Geoff Capes – and get away with it! High jinks during a sports day in the early 1980s.

YOU in the picture

Hands together for *Workers' Playtime*, a radio programme produced by the BBC for the Light Service in factories and mills all over the UK. These happy workers are listening to the acts in the canteen of a company in Portwood, during 1959.

Another edition of *Workers' Playtime* using local entertainers. This programme was produced at R. Gregg & Co, Reddish, during May 1976.

Pupils of Cherry Tree Primary with the very first computer to be used by the school. Most schools now have mega-memory, high speed processor computers. This amazing machine in 1980 was the first home computer, a Clive Sinclair product called the ZX80, with a tiny amount of memory and software loaded from a tape-recorder. Despite its shortcomings the pupils were obviously proud to be in at the start of the white heat of technology.

Janet Abnzi, of Hawk Green, was just one of the worldwide army of fans devoted to the 1970s group The Bay City Rollers. Pictured in October 1977, Janet is surrounded by hundreds of pictures on her bedroom wall.

Head of St Winifred's RC School, Sister Aquinas, together with *Coronation Street* stars Bill Tarmey and Helen Worth. Sister Aquinas retired in 1993 and thought the press and TV cameras were at the school to film the school choir who had previously recorded hits such as *Matchstalk Men* and *There's No One Quite Like Grandma* – she was in fact greeted by a *This is Your Life* film crew, complete with presenter Michael Aspel.

'Claire and Friends'. Pictured in the 1980s are pupils of St Winifred's Primary School, who made a record with the memorable title of *It's hard being in love when you are eight and a half*. Not exactly a hit, but full points for the title! Pictured from the left are: Caroline Conway, Bernard Williams, Claire Usher, Catherine Campfield and Geraldine Lyons.

Out in force for the 1977 Stockport Carnival are these champions of the Hillgate Pram Race.

Local historian Steve Cliffe examines the original carved staircase in the Staircase Café on Stockport Market Place, during 1987. Mr Cliffe, who edits the *Stockport Heritage* magazine, was a staunch campaigner for the restoration of the building.

Danny Murray, a regular at the Windsor Castle, Marple Bridge, takes the 'Pub's Save Water' campaign to heart, during a spell of hot weather in August 1995.

Entrants in the Miss United Biscuits competition regional heat, during an evening in the early 1980s, at the Poco A Poco club (now demolished) Heaton Chapel.

Strictly not politically correct in recent times, but the Miss Stockport competition was an annual event for many years. Pictured is this line-up are the finalists of the 1982 competition.

The Miss Stockport competition of 1988. Bill Tarmey from *Coronation Street* is standing in the centre of the group.

Obviously a friendly encounter, judging from the smile on the face of this pikeman during a Civil War re-enactment in Woodbank Park in May 1990.

Lyme Park became a battleground for an American Civil war re-enactment, as can be seen from this 1980s photograph. An armistice must have been signed as the Confederate and Northern troops seem very happy in each other's company – perhaps they had all been to the Ram's Head in Disley, before the battle.

Stars in the making? Jane Hutchinson and Susan Robinson were given roles in *Coronation Street* during the 1970s. The young lady (centre) was playing in the street and decided to join in as our photographer was taking the picture.

Warm weather during August 1984, produced a story about drivers letting their attention be on things other than driving! This picture was fabricated to fit the story before the days when this would be considered both sexist and contrived. Things have changed, but we stood guilty as charged in 1984!

Romiley Young Farmers' Show is often blighted by bad weather. The year 1996 proved to be an exception with clear blue skies and weather so warm that this particular 'ship of the desert' felt very much at home. Pictured is Cathy Burke of Romiley during the camel race.

'Every Englishman's home is his castle.' Taking this maxim literally is Phil Revington, who built his own, in the garden of his house in Bramhall, in May 2000.

'Hello Mum!' Dave Cunliffe absails from the roof of Stockport College for charity in 1992.

Wine judge John Swait lends an expert nose to the serious business of judging a red wine, during the annual wine and beer show, held at Heald Green Village Hall, 2002.

Marple's Nick Sanders has featured many times in the pages of our newspapers. In a series of constant adventures he has cycled around the world, cycled across the Sahara, just to mention a few of his projects. In our picture Nick checks his navigation as he takes an *Express* photographer across the Peak District moors in a hot air balloon!

We are certain of the time – but uncertain of the date! Ladies of Bramhall Telephone Exchange try not to get their wires crossed, perhaps in the late 1960s or early 1970s?

The Vintage Motor Cycle Club's 50th anniversary rally, starting from the Robin Hood, High Lane, in May 1996. Pictured in the foreground is 85-year-old Harold Pass with his three-wheeler Morgan, which he has owned since 1936.

Gay Liberation march through Stockport in the early 1980s.

A happy demonstration judging from the smiles. CND members campaign outside the old Magistrates Court, Warren Street, for the scrapping of Cruise missiles in 1982.

A drag hunt passes the George Hotel, Compstall, in the early 1980s.

Mel Thorley has appeared several times in the pages of the *Stockport Express* over the years. Mr Thorley is a train driver and one of the Stockport's characters. He has an amazing enthusiasm for railways, even buying a house next to a railway line! Mel is pictured with just some of his garden ornaments.

Floods near the Jack and Jill pub at Brinnington around 1970. Where is that beautiful E-Type Jaguar now? In a dry heated garage we hope.

A picture taken in February 2002 shows Mrs Patricia Kidd and fellow resident Geoff Earnshaw paddling to their homes through floodwaters on Cawood Square, Brinnington.

Another soaking for our photographer as children make the best of flooding in the Gatley Green area in April 1969.

Were you the small boy with his finger in the dyke? This mysterious picture was found in an archive folder marked 'Floods'. Apart from the 92 bus to Hazel Grove, we are also uncertain of the location.

We are uncertain of the exact date for this photograph just captioned 'Floods – Hazel Grove' in our files. We would guess the late 1960s judging from the long hair of the gentleman in the picture. The lady with the curlers (right) seems ready to attack the floods with a vacuum cleaner!

High winds during December 2001 left these scaffolders with some extra work. Originally the scaffolding was on the opposite wall. Becoming detached it came to rest against this wall on Bridge Street Brow, leading to the Market Place.

Not a very happy day for the driver of this bus bringing visitors to the Lyme Festival in the 1980s. Apparently the Crossville breakdown crew had to be helped by the army to free the double-decker as it leaned on to the stone pillar, nearly sending the proud eagle crashing to the floor!

Lyme Horse trials, September 1991. Miss Caroline Row on *Rosscarne* stay together on this demanding course.

1890s? No, the picture was taken in 1990 to reproduce a Victorian scene at Lyme Hall. In our picture are housemaid Mrs Carol Bell and housekeeper Mrs Jean Coulthurst, cleaning an armour-clad gentleman who is displaying the same proud expression for our photographer as he did for the original artist!

Another replica period Lyme photograph, taken in 1992. These children of estate workers donned authentic dress for our photographer to advertise a forthcoming Edwardian day.

Stockport's Elmfield Brass Band has the honour to play in the new bandstand at Vernon Park in May 2000.

Admiring a high-level view of the now demolished site of Simon Engineering in Birdhall Lane in the early 1980s is former *Stockport Express* journalist Graham Dudman. Graham was treated to a ride in a Simon Super Snorkel which was produced for the fire services. He has gone on to an even more elevated position as the assistant editor of *The Sun* newspaper.

Street Works – Stockport's international street festival parade in Merseyway during May 2001.

'Ole' – a motorised 'bull' keeps people amused, during the Street Works, Stockport's international street festival parade in Merseyway, 2001.

Street festival in Stockport town centre in 1996.

Nina Newbury (aged 11) of Woodhall Road, South Reddish, with a 1968 Mini covered in pennies, at Penny Lane, Heaton Norris. The car was on its way to a show in Manchester in 1996

A three-hour line dancing marathon at Romiley Forum in 1997.

The start of the Bullock Smithy hike in 1993.

Anybody for a sandwich? This signwriter was obviously thinking of his lunch when he completed this sign on the M60. For strangers to the town, BREADbury should be written as Bredbury.

Residents of Mellor were obviously getting tired of these tunneling operations as some wag has added this 'escape' sign.

'Oh Mummy!' Kirsty McDermott (11), from Bredbury, was taking part in a Vernon Park Museum trail in February 2002 when she came across one of the clues, which was a real mummy's hand in a box.

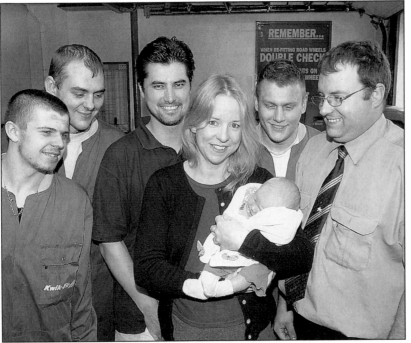

Delivering 100 per cent customer satisfaction: Kwik Fit fitters who helped to deliver baby Bronte Louise in the firm's car park at Heaton Lane in 2001. Pictured with the fitters are proud parents. 'You can't get better than a Kwik Fit nipper!' These pictures and story were one of several from the *Stockport Express* that were judged as a complete package of stories and pictures earning the newspaper the title of Best Weekly Newspaper in the North during the BT Regional Media Awards in May 2002.

Sub-district	Stockport
1.	**Date and place of birth** Second August 2001 Kwik-Fit Car Park, Heaton Lane,
2.	**Name and surname** Bronte Louise MacMILLAN

Bronte's birth certificate, confirming the place she chose to come into the world – the Kwik Fit car park!